Introduction

Thank you for purchasing the book *Kindle Self-Publishing Tips – 25+ Untold Tips Which Will Maximize Your Profits By 300%.*

I'm sure that you have bought a lot of Kindle Publishing Books that have nothing new to say.

This book provides 25+ tips for maximizing your profits, all of which come from my own experience.

You will learn:

- How to promote your book
- When the best periods to promote your book are
- The benefits of publishing your book in multiple formats
- The importance of KDP Select
- How to maximize your profits by 300%
- Illustrations and proof to accompany most of the tips
- Charts from my own account
- A lot more useful tips based on my own experiences

Tip #1 – Don't use all of your Free Promo days at once

If you have decided to promote your book using KDP Select (the 5 free days every 90 days), don't use all the days at once, spread them into a series of 1 or 2 days maximum.

Why?

Because Amazon has a different number of customers each day. For the same book, I experienced excellent days which brought me nearly 700 free units in one day and periods when that book brought me just 40-50 free units.

I know it's easier to schedule the days all at once, but it isn't too profitable. Because of those free units, your book ranks higher in the searches and people will start seeing your book, they will find you easier. If you manage to reach 200 free units in one day, the next day you will start selling at least 1 unit each day and even get borrows for it – guaranteed 100%.

Let me give you an example and then I will show you proof – if you don't "choose" your best days or you schedule your book to be free when it's the worst period and use them all at once, you will get 200-350 units in total (for all 5 days). If you put it for 1 day and you get a boom of 200 free units in that day, it's enough to boost it in the rankings and it will start generating money.

It's advisable to use the remaining days when you see that your sales are starting to drop (for that book).

Proof:

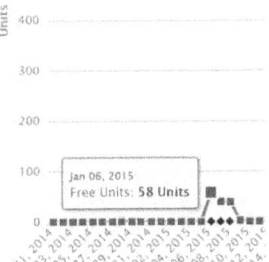

When I used the book in 2 series – 3 days in a row and after a few days 2 days in a row I got interesting results. As I said, each day, the market is different. I got 58 units, 48, and 42 – not too good, so in total almost 150 free units.

After a few days, I used the last 2 days and I had outstanding results – 71 free units the first day and the second day – 697 free units.

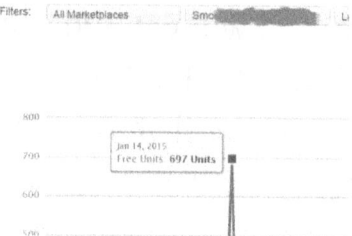

This is only for 1 book, I won't share its name publicly.

Imagine if I had that day from the beginning and had 4 more additional days. Let me show you the sales after that last day with excellent results. The promo was on the 6th, 7th and 8th of January. Soon after...1 sale/day on average.

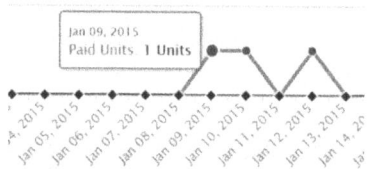

But after the boom of 697 free units in one single day, the results were like this:

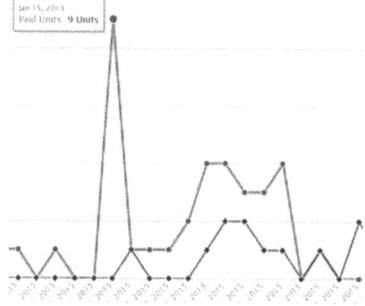

This will give you an idea of how important the number of free units is and why it is advisable to use them wisely. In this case, I have used 2 in a row and 3 in a row. Try to use them 1 day or 2 days, no more than that.

Tip #2 – Promote your books from Sunday to Thursday

Promoting your books is crucial for obtaining profits. There are days in which there are not too many customers/readers on Amazon.

When is the best day to promote your book?

From Sunday to Thursday. I've noticed that on Sundays you get the best results and on Fridays and Saturdays you get the worst results.

The reason is because people usually go shopping, they travel, go out to the clubs, cinemas etc. they don't stay online on Amazon to buy your books (seriously, on Friday evening you start reading?).

In case you have the luck to sell any books or get any free units during promotions on Fridays and Saturdays, you will get them in the evening or while you are asleep. Some users still surf Amazon and grab a book to read before they go to bed at 1:00 – 3:00 AM.

I had days when I haven't sold one single copy (Saturday), and the next day (Sunday) I had the best day of the month. It came as a surprise.

Tip #3 – Make a Paperback Version

As soon as you finish your book, make sure to upload it first on CreateSpace (if you want a Paperback version). It will give customers the possibility to buy a physical book or a Kindle book – it's their choice.

The paperback version also gives more credibility and it will boost your sales. If you use their recommended file size (.doc) which is 6" x 9" it will increase your number of pages.

CreateSpace
Digital print publishing
made easy

ACX
Print audiobook publishing
made easy

I don't know how other people look for books, but if it was up to me...I wouldn't bother buying books of 15 – 20 pages. In my opinion, a book has to have at least 30-40 pages (even though I have one book which has 25 pages). So, increasing the number of pages (by writing and by format) will also boost your sales.

For the same book, on a standard A4 size from Microsoft Word, I got 41 pages.

After I have set the page size to 6" x 9" (recommended print size from CreateSpace) I managed to get 66 pages.

I'm not saying now to write 10 pages and make 100 out of them, but just to boost a little bit to attract more readers.

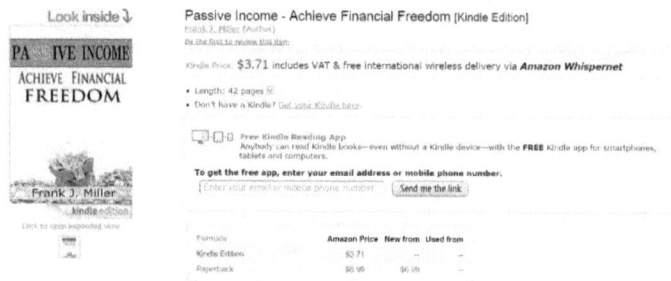

As I said, Paperback books will appear in the other format as shown in the picture. This gives readers more credibility.

Uploading your book on CreateSpace is easy, but you have to have your content ready and your cover finished. As soon as it's uploaded, there is a link directly to KDP and they will automatically link your book there.

And most important of all, it's free to upload.

Tip #4 - Create Bundles

Every time you start writing a new book, keep in mind the idea that it's better to make a similar idea so you can mix that book to another one and create a bundle – maximize profits.

If you create 10 books about Paleo for example – Paleo Salads, Paleo Desserts, Paleo Breakfasts, Paleo Crockpot Recipes, Paleo Sauces, Paleo Seafood, Paleo Smoothies, Paleo Fish, Paleo Slow Cooker Recipes and Paleo Soups you can mix them together in 2,3...10 books, but for a lower price.

If you write all of them with 30 recipes and an in-depth introduction and write around 40-50 pages for each book and price them at 2.99$, for 2 books you can price them at 3.99$ (instead of 5.99$), 5 books for 5.99$ (instead of 14.99$) and 10 books for 7.99$ (instead of 29.99$). You can make 5 bundles of 2, 5 bundles of 3, 3 bundles of 5 and 1 bundle of 10 books.

After all, it's a bargain to buy a 10in1 book which as almost 500 pages, around 300 recipes and it costs 7.99$.

If you get in average 30$ for 1 book, you will have in total 10 books (individual) + 5 bundles of 2 + 5 bundles of 3 + 3 bundles of 5 and + 1 of 10 which is 10 + 5 + 5 + 3 + 1 = 24 books, so you have created 14 additional books out of 10.

If you would have sold just the 10 books, you would have got 300$ a month and if you would have mixed them in bundles like in the example, you would have got 24 x 30$ = 720$ / month.

That's a 140% increase in the number of books and profits.

I use bundles too, they're profitable.

Tip #5 – Rewrite your own books

I don't know if you have noticed, but if somebody uploads a good book, you will see the refunds will appear in your dashboard, negative reviews without any sense and in a few months, your sales drop because a lot of similar books appear in the searches. Some of them with 99% the same title as yours.

Guess why?

Some competitors steal your ideas, even content – they buy and refund, or download when it's free and then copy your work (they rewrite it).

So...what if...I would rewrite my own books, with even more pages, explanations, but have the same thing as the previous ones – you only change the cover and the Pen Name. You will then compete you with yourself and it will be a lot harder for others to compete with you for the same niche.

I think this is a smart way to avoid competition or to recover your sales if they started dropping.

Some people are really a pain in the back. I usually write good quality books and I write the books by myself, I don't pay writers even if I could do that. I get good reviews from people and suddenly I see 2 reviews of 1 star on the same book and both of them were unverified reviews – they didn't actually buy the book or at least downloaded it for free.

Those people are competitors, they give bad reviews so you will experience a sales drop. If you drop your sales, they will take the lead and so on. It's like in the jungle, but this is the truth. I don't mind reading a review of 2 stars which was a verified purchase and it has a reason for that review, a detailed description of the PROs and CONs, but it just says something like "I didn't like it" or "Poor quality" which is inconclusive.

Rewriting your own books and changing the pen name will increase profits and reduce competition.

Tip #6 – Use your own ideas

When you write new books, don't just rewrite content and books that sell, use your imagination and experience too, your own ideas and what you actually have to say. People will love that.

If you were a customer and wanted to read something new about meditation, you would find 100 books with recycled content, not too many new ideas. There probably are some well-written books with a lot of pages and which provide new information, but there are very few.

From my experience, even though it is less than 1 year since I have started publishing books in Kindle, I have noticed that books in which I put out my ideas maintain in the rankings for a longer period and they get better reviews too.

Try to use your personal thoughts when you write books, even if they are fiction or nonfiction ones.

Tip #7 – Vote for reviews

When you get positive reviews vote them "Yes" at the section "Was this review helpful to you?" and "No" for the negative ones.

It will put up the ones with the biggest number of "Yes" votes and it will drop down the ones with the biggest number of "No" votes. It will help you keep the best reviews up and customers will be able to see them.

☆☆☆☆☆ **Getting ready to promote your book?** February 26, 2015
By Suzanne Dean
Verified Purchase

This book gives you many ideas of where to promote your book, a couple that my research didn't find. The author also warns what is good to do, and what to avoid. A schedule of how to, and what to do calendar and the actions to prepare for your promo in advance. After reading this book I realized that you can promote without spending money, but be prepared to spend a few dollars if you really need to get your name out there. Overall, I found this book to be a quick read, to the point, and informative

Comment | Was this review helpful to you? Yes No

As a customer, you wouldn't like to see the first reviews of the book being negative. Some negative reviews may be real and you should ask yourself why you got them, but some of them are given by haters or competitors. Every book gets negative reviews, even the best ones – there has to be someone who doesn't like something.

Tip #8 – Set up Author Central

Set up an account on Author Central on Amazon. Write something about yourself and upload a photo of you. Don't worry, you can still use your Pen Names in parallel with your real name.

Publish books under your real name too, people will see clearly who is the Author and what kind of books is he writing.

It's advisable also to create a website and make a back-end business out of your books. A back-end business should have other courses, affiliate links, Google AdWords and other profitable things.

By setting the Author Central page, you will boost your overall sales.

Tip #9 – Choose descriptive titles and subtitles

It's very important when you upload your book to choose a good title, it has to be descriptive and to say in few words what readers will actually find in your book.

Write at least one benefit and what the book contains.

It is also important to include a lot of keywords in it.

Example: *How to start a business from home – 10 proven online income streams that will bring you financial freedom*

Even if the title is long, it has keywords – "How to start a business"; "Hot to start a business from home"; " Proven methods for achieving financial freedom" etc. and you can clearly see the benefit – financial freedom and money.

Bad title example: *30 KDP tips* – what do you understand from that? I don't understand anything, it has to be descriptive.

You can also add "How to" or "know how" segments. It will be eye catching.

Do the same for the subtitle, add something descriptive as well, don't leave the space blank.

You have a word limit for setting your title and subtitle. It is advisable to push it to the limit, use as many keywords as possible, but to make sense.

Tip #10 – Create a series of books

If you have multiple ideas, don't waste them all on one book, spread them out into a series of books (of 50 pages each), add details, your opinion, outsource some content and upload them.

Of course, as soon as you finish your series of books, you can add a bundle, as I have mentioned earlier.

This will increase your earnings, as you can promote them individually and let people borrow them individually.

Include keywords in the series' title as well, keywords that are different from the title and subtitle.

Tip #11 – Choose the best keywords

It's very important to choose the best keywords for your book so you can maximize your number of readers.

First of all, include keywords in your title (see the title and subtitle tip), in your series title and the other 7 keywords that Amazon lets you use.

Use the keywords with the optimum number of results – it must be not to narrow and not too broad. What I am referring to is that you have to get somewhere between 300 and 1000 results for a keyword. If it has more than that – 1500-2000 results or more it's too broad, people will find your book really hard. If it's too narrow – it has around 50 results, it's too broad – there is not enough market for your keyword (book).

Pick the ones that are between 300 and 1000. For example, for my book *How to start a business from home* – this is a keyword and it is directly in the title. For that keyword, I get 306 results and it is at the top of the list. I have put this keyword for other books of mine as it has proven to be profitable.

Tip #12 – Make audible versions of the book

Kindle stands for digital formats, CreateSpace for Paperback versions and Audible ACX makes your book ready for Audible versions.

It's indicated to make an audio version for your book as you increase your sales, profits, and credibility.

The only problem is that when you make this version, it isn't free like the Paperback version. You have to pay a narrator to professionally narrate your book and make a voice over. You will also have to provide rights for the audio content which will charge you even more.

What books should you make with Audible versions? I think the best ones are for Kids – Children's books. Any parent would buy a bedtime story, but it's tiring to read books all the time for your children. Even if it's lovely to stay watch your child hearing you and asking you all kinds of funny questions, you will surely have nights when you are pissed off, bored or very tired and your child wants to hear a bedtime story. So what do you do? You buy the audio version and he can listen to it how many times he wants.

Business books are also welcome for Audible versions and as well as Fiction books, especially novellas.

If you want to invest in something new and profitable, try out the Audio versions.

The main disadvantage is that it is only for publishers from US or UK (the author's location).

CreateSpace
Indie print publishing
made easy

ACX
Indie audiobook publishing
made easy

Tip #13 – Change your cover and keywords if the book is not selling

You may experience to work hard for a book, you design or buy a cover, you promote your book using KDP Select and at the end you won't see too fancy results.

What do you do?

I hope you didn't think about getting your book unpublished. You just have to change the cover, keywords and re-promote it. It will be shortly revived.

You can also do that if you see a drop in sales. Leave the content as it was previously. Don't change it.

Tip #14 – Update your book after each negative review

You will surely get negative reviews of 1 and 2 stars, it's inevitable. There must be haters and competitors out there.

In some cases, those reviews reflect reality – maybe your book has errors, lack of information or it's just useless.

If you see that negative reviews are pouring, reread your book and add details, correct errors and add more pages to it.

Also, try to leave comments for your reviews and vote no for them so they can drop down.

Tip #15 – Update your books which are profitable

If you wrote a book of 40 pages and it's priced at 2.99$ and you see that nice results are pouring, add 20-30 pages more, illustrations, and new chapters.

Improve your book, bring it to its best and increase the price also. Your profits will increase exponentially.

If you wrote a book of 30-40 pages and you don't see good results, change its cover and keywords. If good results start rolling in, improve it and maximize profits.

In other words, each book that you have has to bring money. Improve it and change it until it brings money.

Some sell better, some don't, but you can try to bring them to their best.

Tip #16 – Enroll in KDP Select

This is probably the most important marketing strategies for Kindle, if you don't enroll in KDP Select you won't be able to promote your book, to sell your books on other Amazon stores (in Europe, Canada, Australia etc.) and you won't be able to lend your book (to receive borrows).

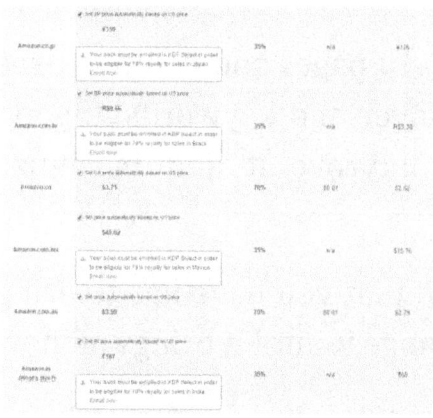

KDP increases profits by over 800%. A book without KDP doesn't sell more than 2-3 copies a month unless you are a popular Author.

KDP give you the possibility to lend your book (for which you receive 1.2 – 1.5$ / borrow – this dropped from 2$/ borrow last year), it also gives you the possibility to promote your book for 5 days – Kindle Countdown Deals or Free Promotion Days.

It gives you a broader audience for your books and you reach more readers and customers.

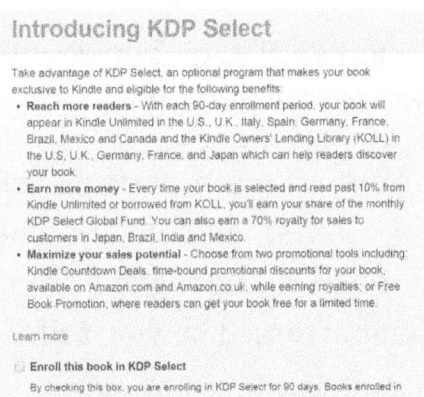

To enroll in KDP Select just tick the box, it will appear at the top each time you will upload a new title.

Tip #17 – Write books under your real name

If you only wrote books using Pen Names, you should definitely try to write a book using your real name.

Make sure the books that you write are perfect – no mistakes, good quality, make sure they deliver value to readers. Remember, the book is under your name and you won't want to get embarrassed by yourself.

Making book under your real name and setting up your Author Central Page will give more credibility to customers and it will be more likely to buy your books.

Write a short biography about yourself and upload it there, people want to know more about the Author, what other books you have for sale, etc.

It's important to combine the Pen Names with your real name – to write books under your name and under pen names.

Tip #18 – Pay for ad campaigns

Amazon recently launched a program which helps you promote your book even more and significantly increase your sales.

In your dashboard, you will see "Ad Campaigns".

Sales Dashboard
View unit sales transactions for current and prior months

Prior Six Weeks' Royalties
View your royalties for the past six weeks

Promotions
View the performance of your Kindle Countdown Deals promotions (updated periodically as your promotion runs).

Ad Campaigns
Manage ad campaigns and check your billing history.

To take advantage of this service, you must create an account on Amazon Marketing Services, which is also through KDP and you can set a certain amount of money that you are willing to invest in for promoting your books.

The minimum amount is 100$ and you will be charged 0.02$/bid for every CPC (cost-per-click).

It is advisable to use this service only for your bestselling books – profits will explode. It's definitely worth it. I tried it for 1 book and from 2-3 sales/day I started to have 6-7 sales/day during that campaign.

So it's a 150% increase in sales for 1 book. If that book costs 2.99$ and my royalty is 2.07$/book, the campaign brings me at least 3-4, let's say 3 sales, which is 6.21$, it means that in 30 days I get 186.30$ from that campaign, which is an 86.30$ profit. The thing is that it may or may not run out of that 100$ initial credit. For 100$, you will get 10,000 cents and for 2 cents/bid you will get 5000 clicks from customers. At least 10-15% will buy if they click.

Imagine if you had more expensive books and you advertise 5-6 books at the same time. You could increase your earnings with 500-600$ at least which is good.

Tip #19 – Include affiliate links in your books

When you publish your books, try to put affiliate links in them. People who are interested in buying something on Amazon, eBay, etc. will click on them and if they buy something through your link, you will get a commission.

For example, you make a book about the iPad – an overall review, characteristics, tips and tricks, etc. I've seen that those books are actually selling. Include affiliate links with the iPad, accessories, etc.

In one year if you give away 2000 free units and sell 200 units (which is 16 books/month – a book every 2 days) you will reach plus borrows, you will reach over 2500 people. From that number, at least 10% which are 250 people will click on it, and 10% from the other 10%, which are 25 people will actually buy an iPad or some accessories through your links. Amazon's Associates program offers commissions from 4 to 10%. If you would get 5% from the iPad's price which is around 399$ in average, maybe even more, you would get 5% from 399$ which is 20$ for a purchase and multiplied by 25 = 500$ in 1 year extra money for including those affiliate links.

To include affiliate links, make an account for Amazon Associates and request your unique links.

It's even more interesting the fact that, if they click on your link with the iPad, but they buy another tablet, you will also get a commission. That's because that customer arrived at that product with the help of your affiliate link.

Try to request and use as many affiliate links as possible, after all you don't have anything to lose.

Tip #20 – Submit your books to free websites

Before you run a free promotion, make sure you submit your books on free websites – there are millions of readers who have subscriptions and they are just waiting for new books to show up. Books like yours.

So, submitting your book to these websites will increase your number of downloads. Thus, your ranking of the book will increase (readers will find it a lot easier). The more downloads, the better it is.

There are some websites which charge you to submit your books, but they guarantee a certain number of downloads. If you have a good book, use that as well.

Tip #21 - Submit your books to Social Media platforms

Before you put your book for free using KDP Select, make sure to submit it to groups on Facebook, Twitter, LinkedIn, etc.

There are closed of readers on certain topics – business, health, recipes, news, etc.

Search for those groups and submit your book, a lot of those people will download your book for free – you will provide them with free information and you rank your book higher in the searches. The more free units you give away, the more sales you will get after the free promotion.

It's advisable to use these platforms and to combine it with the previous tip, to use free websites. You will increase your free units download rate with at least 50% using these 2 simple methods.

Tip #22 – Enroll in Kindle Matchbook

If you have already released new Paperback books, make sure you have enrolled in Kindle Matchbook – this will allow customers who buy your paperback version to get the Digital format for free, for 0.99$ or for 1.99$. I use Kindle Matchbook, but I give the book for free if they buy the Paperback version.

It's a unique way to attract more customers, a logo appears when they access my books (you have probably seen it before buying this book)

Tip #23 – Worst periods of the month

If you experience drops in sales from 14th to 23rd of the month, don't worry, it's normal to be that way. I have noticed that for a few months consecutively, that period is always dropping sales. This is mainly caused by the fact that people get paid around 20th to 25th and until they get their money on their credit cards, they won't make too many purchases. The same thing applies for borrows. Here is two examples from my charts:

For January:

For March:

Another reason is that Kindle Unlimited (KU) subscriptions expire and they have to pay another one which is 9.99$/month.

There also periods when you won't even make free units, not too many people surf Amazon each day.

Saturdays are also awful days for selling, promoting or marketing – people are out for shopping, traveling, having fun, etc.

Tip #24 – Hire a virtual assistant

If you want to promote your book, write books faster, submit them to websites, but you don't have any time, hire yourself a VA.

A virtual assistant will charge you around 2-3$/hour and you can give him 3-4 hours a day to work which is let's say 2.5$/hour x 4 hours a day x 25 days = 250$/month.

It may sound a lot, but while he is promoting your books and submitting them to websites, you can write new books and stop wasting precious time.

Of course, this task should be done when you earn at least 1,000$/month from KDP and you can afford that VA.

If your business is growing even further, you can hire multiple VAs.

You can find virtual assistants on http://freelancer.com or http://odesk.com or http://elance.com

Tip #25 – Hire ghostwriters for outsourcing

If you want to outsource a new subject which you want to write about and you don't have too many ideas, pay a ghostwriter to write down some ideas for you.

The price is somewhere around 3-5$/500-750 words for which you can get a list of ideas which you can then develop and detail by yourself.

If you have enough money, you can use ghostwriters to write your whole book and you just have to proofread it (or hire somebody else to proofread it).

Errors are something that customers don't like, but in spite of this, there is no perfect book. Even the mightiest writers have their own errors or mistakes. It just happens.

You can find writers on http://iWriter.com or http://odesk.com or http://fiverr.com or http://elance.com or http://freelancer.com

Tip #26 – The most important tip for Kindle:

PERSEVERANCE

Writing books on Kindle won't make you rich overnight, you have to work hard to achieve your goals, to maximize profits and to achieve financial freedom. It's a long-term process which I haven't managed to reach yet.

Perseverance is the most powerful thing in this world, there is a famous quote for that:

"Nothing in the world can take the place of persistence. Talent will not; nothing is more common than unsuccessful men with talent. Genius will not; unrewarded genius is almost a proverb. Education will not; the world is full of educated derelicts. Persistence and determination alone are omnipotent. The slogan "Press On!" has solved and always will solve the problems of the human race." - *Calvin Coolidge*

Conclusion

Thank you once again for purchasing and reading this book. I hope you will be able to increase your earnings after reading each of the tips that I have written.

All of the tips are based on true facts, on the experience that I have accumulated over the past few months.

If the book has meant something for you, I kindly ask you to write a short review for it so I can improve my books and me as a person.

Thank you

Kindest regards,

Frank